TOOKIE BEAR

25 YEARS MARRIED TO JULIA:
REFLECTIONS A-Z ON BEING AND
STAYING MARRIED

DOUG SERVEN

For Julie
My Tookie Bear

CONTENTS

PRACTICALLY ENGAGED (BUT NOT YET)

A POEM WRITTEN THE NIGHT BEFORE THE PROPOSAL

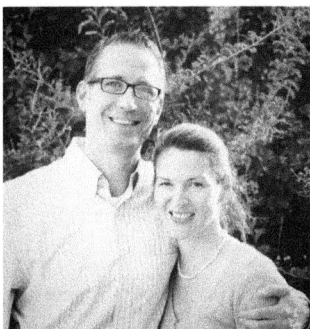

2012

Yes, I'm nervous. Probably won't sleep
Don't know how to get up to the cross
Might lose the ring between now and then
May part my hair on the wrong side
Or sleepwalk
And she'll see me too soon.
Need some 1 Peter 5:7 for sure

Or some major drugs
(Too many Clearly Canadians)
No really, I'm fine
Proverbs 2:8 and tomorrow is coming
Hooray

August 14, 1993

58 DAYS

A POEM I WROTE BEFORE WE WERE MARRIED

2015—decked out!

Only once will I stand to marry her
I've never become one before
One one half, at .5 speed, 1/2 force
Never again

I remember the bridge where the
First I love you arrived scared and
Confident
Finally returned, sealing our coming
I've said those words many times since
But always they mean more
Deeper bigger fuller richer
But I'll never marry her again
And she's the difference
One time one shot
One day to bend our life together
At four fifteen I'll stand with C Mitchell
At four sixteen with my wife
Before God Almighty in his hands
I'm scared and confident again
But this is no escalator first kiss
In fifty-eight days
The once begins

January 6, 1994

VOW

March 5, 1994

Julie, I love you. I believe it was God's total and sovereign will that brought us together at the John-ston Dining Hall, and that it is his will that we become one together in Christ.

I promise to serve and lead you, to respect and honor you, and to make your life an adventure each and every second.
I joyfully take you to be my beloved wife (and Pootie Pie).

26 WORDS TO DESCRIBE HER

A TO Z

AMBROSIAL

At Silver Dollar City when we were dating

Ambrosial is a fancy word for delightful. Julie has become more and more delightful in the years I have known her. We met in the dorms at Mizzou our sophomore year. We lived in the men's and women's dorms (Johnston and Wolpers), and they shared a small dining hall. Everyone in these two dorms gathered every night for supper.

We had mutual friends and were introduced. Nice to meet you, but not much more.

The next morning, I saw her as I set out to class. We realized we'd met the night before, and that we had the same class together, so we walked there with each other.

It seemed awkward to get there and then not sit near each other. So we did. I remember it was in the Geography department, but I can't recall which class it was.

After class, I stood up to say goodbye, and we then realized we had the same next class together. Since we were both sophomore journalism majors, we had nearly the exact same schedule. So we started walking together and sitting together, and then eating together and studying together.

I was delighted. She was ambrosial.

But here's the thing—she's even more ambrosial now. She's nearing peak ambrosial I think, though I'm not sure how it's possible to go down. She's more interesting, more funny, more pretty, more cool, and more just about everything I want.

I'm so thankful I met her in the fall of 1990, and that we've stuck it out.

BESPECKLED

March 5, 1994

We always joked that we hoped our kids got my teeth and her eyes.

I've had glasses since I was in third grade. I'd sit six inches away from the tv screen because that was the only way I could see it. I grew up with nerdy glasses and even nerdier Rec Specs. I had contacts, and lasik surgery and then back to glasses again, and I give up.

But I had good teeth. I prided myself on my zero cavities record, which lasted well into my forties.

Julie has had the opposite. She has a mouth full of silver colors. But her eyes were perfect.

Then they weren't. This is a process of aging of course. It's not a moral problem or sign of neglect or bad living.

It's not a big deal that she needs reading glasses, but I'm glad to have gotten to see her admit her need, and then get a certain amount of help (this is true for depression too).

She sure looks cute in those glasses, and she's been wearing them more.

CHEEKY

Recreating the proposal at Eagle Lake Camp

Julie's sense of humor is a little understated. If you didn't know better, you might think she is straight-laced and buttoned up.

I think that's because she had some (relatively)

wild years in junior high and high school. When we met in college she was a hard-charging young woman who wanted to work at a major news network, probably an editor for NBC or CBS or ABC.

She also wasn't a Christian when we met. I remember asking her about Christianity, and she didn't have many answers. It was a big blank spot.

I didn't exactly handle this well. I broke up with her one night by drawing an illustration on a piece of paper that explained that I knew I was going to be in heaven with Jesus, and she had eternal damnation in her future. Not good. Not good.

On the other hand, I talked about my beliefs and hers, and my faith mattered to me. I made a ton of mistakes because I'm both a sinner and a big dummy, but Jesus seemed to make a difference in my life. That intrigued her.

Julie came to trust in Jesus as her Savior too.

What does this have to do with cheeky? As a serious, career-minded young woman who had just come to faith in Christ, she had a lot to learn and change and grow in. She wanted to follow Christ and his commands. She wanted to be a "good" girl-friend and then wife and then mother. Life changed a lot for her in quick order. Graduating, moving to Stillwater, marriage, pregnancy, mother-hood, more moving, more changing, more pregnan-cies, more life...

I'm just trying to say that she didn't have as much space as she does now to be as sassy as she is. People don't know this about her, but the sass is strong within her. And I love that part.

DISSIMILAR

City Pres photo booth

I could say either Dissimilar or Differentiated. Both would work.

I think men and women share much/most in common. Our internal organs aren't that different. We're most the same in our blood and brains, our hearts, and our veins.

Julie and I both grew up in small towns in Missouri in the 1970s and '80s. We both ended up at Mizzou as journalism majors, and we lived in the same dorm. We had the same schedule.

But then things also diverge. I grew up in the church (for good and bad), but she didn't. My parents stayed married (and still are), but hers divorced when she was not yet a teenager.

For a long time, we tested out as me an ENFP and her an ISTJ (though she's changed her tune and now says she's an INFP).

Our lives joined up, so we've become more similar I suppose. We share more interests, like how now we both care about rowing because two of our kids row. We care about Charlottesville and UVA because our daughter and her husband live and work there. We care about film and social media because our son and his wife do. We started a publishing company, so we both care about editing books, whereas previously that was her forte and something I left behind. Sometimes I can get her to play a board game with me.

Same-ness is cool. We've built a life together. It's 25 years in for marriage, but another three before that.

The word is Dissimilar though.

I like how she's different. We're not the same.

My biggest enjoyment is her femininity. I hope not to be in TMI land, so you can read between the lines. I'm a cis-gendered heterosexual man, and I'm crazy about her as a woman. I like her curves and lines and smoothness. I like trying to figure her out, as crazy as that makes me sometimes. I like making her happy, as often as I fail.

I have a WWJD wonder. What Would Julie Do? I know what she'd do is better than my natural instinct, so if I can at least think about it, I'm more on the right track.

Differentiated is a more psychological word that means that our lives are overlapping and involved but not enmeshed. She can still be her, and I can still be me. She can like yoga, and I can like CrossFit. And then a few years later, I can like yoga, and she can like CrossFit. We can have different interests and thoughts.

But we're on the same team.

ECCLESIAL

Red Andrews Dinner, Christmas Day 2016

Julie didn't know she was marrying a pastor because I wasn't one when we were dating. Or newly married.

I grew up in the church. I had perfect attendance pins. But I'm not sure I loved God or Christ. It will be interesting to find out my conversion date. I do know that something changed my freshman year in college in the spring.

I'd moved into the dorms, and I met people involved in a group called The Navigators. Several of these guys had moved into the dorms as seniors in college. They'd given up whatever privileges they'd had in their fraternities or groups in order to be around freshmen like me, grouped two by two, bathing in communal showers. It wasn't the high life by any means.

[This isn't meant to be a book about me, but about her, but I know my story better than hers, so they're intertwined.]

That's where I met Brad, Matt, Dan, Al, Bob, and others. They were my friends. And they loved Jesus. They memorized Scripture, read the Bible, talked about God, tried to follow God's commands, and they were a part of The Navigators. So I was too.

That made a big difference in my life. This was my tribe, the people I ran around with. That may seem strange, but it's not that different than any other tribe or group.

So, when I graduated, I "went on staff" with The Navigators. That means I joined their group as what I'd call and intern or apprentice. I was placed in Stillwater at Oklahoma State University. I wanted to help college students like I'd been helped.

Julie also moved to Stillwater and started work for a small tech company. We were engaged, then married, and then she was pregnant a month later.

Shifts happened as we tried to figure out a new marriage, a premature daughter in Tulsa, a changing theology, a life below the poverty line, and a call to ministry.

I ended up in St Louis at seminary, and then at the University of Oklahoma. I was ordained as a minister in the Presbyterian Church in America on September 16, 2001, yes five days after 9/11.

We had bought a house in June, our first one. We'd had our fourth child, Anna, in August.

This was a whirlwind. And Julie was married to a pastor. How did that happen? I told her she was a lucky woman....

I'm sure I'll get to other parts of the story, but I've got to skip ahead.

After ten years in campus ministry at the University of Oklahoma, I helped start City Presbyterian Church in Oklahoma City. I helped start it with Rev. Bobby Griffith as my wingman. And our wives—Julie and Jennifer.

Starting a church (church planting) is rough. It's hard to explain. I think it's a mix of being a doctor, a lawyer, and an entrepreneur, but then you have to mix in all the religious components, and then not having any idea what you're doing, along with not exactly being trained to start a church.

One of our (me and Bobby's) goals was that our wives didn't hate the church. We wanted Julie and Jennifer to be free to enjoy it, not burdened under the pressure to what people think pastors' wives should be. So we didn't sign them up for nursery, or women's ministry, or speaking, or even hosting.

I think it's worked. I suppose you'd have to ask her. Julie (and Jennifer) have been through the wringer no doubt.

We couldn't have done without them. They've believed in us, and the church. They've contributed in a million ways to make it better and better. They've given their blood, sweat, and tears, but most of the time gladly bearing these burdens as followers of Christ.

Julie LOVES people. She's so good at it. If you get to meet her and spend time with her, you are blessed beyond measure. She'll be your friend, your confidant, your advocate, your ride, your greeter, your rebuker, your build-upper. She's all in for church, because she loves Jesus and his church.

FOXY

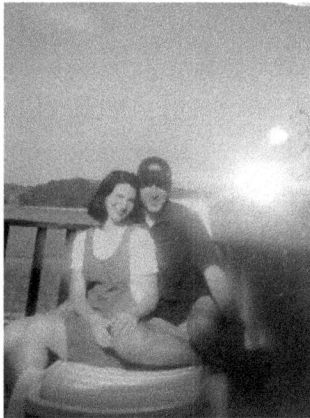

*Our one year wedding anniversary trip at Grand
Lake in Oklahoma*

Foxy. I considered waiting for this one until Vulpine.

One of our jokes is that when it's the day before her birthday, I tell her that I'm attracted to women X years old. This year I'll say, "I'm really attracted to 47 year old women." [I don't mean ALL 47-year-old women, just her.]

But then in the morning, I'll say, "I've changed my mind from last night. I'm flipping over to 48-year-old women." She'll say, "Whew."

I think she's prettier now than when we met. We met when we were nineteen.

I turned twenty while she was nineteen We were exactly six months apart, which means my half birthday is her birthday, which means my half birthday gets ignored. Her birthday is also Cinco De Mayo. She also likes cheap Mexican food, places that are slammed that day. I've convinced her finally that we can do a take out order that's amazing and share it with friend. Or we can go into actual real Mexican restaurants in communities where Cinco de Mayo isn't an Americanized holiday, and the food is better too.

When I turned 20, I had six months of hazing on her. No matter what she'd do or say, I always had a side glance, a rolling of the eyes, and I'd say, "Ugh. Teenagers...." I'd start every conversation with, "Well, as a teenager, it's obvious you'd think that, but as an adult, I'll teach you the ways of the world. "

This was a serious miscalculation. I had my one decade of "glory."

However, we ended up together. So now when I entered my 30s, she was still in her 20s for another six months. I had that same six months in my 40s while she stayed in her 30s. The 50s-40s is quickly approaching. I guess it's worth it. I deserve it. I didn't think ahead.

I can't imagine a foxier wife than her. She's super sexy. And going to CrossFit to improve that cute butt she has.

I'm going to like her in her 50s, 60s, 70s. and 80s as my tastes in women change.

GRAVID

*From a wedding we attended—Megan and
Squeaks?—mid-early 2000s*

When Julie and I were engaged, we started talking
about something I had never thought about before.
We were soon going to able to and responsible for
bringing souls into the world. That blew my mind.

We considered our options, and we threw out
many of them. We settled on perhaps the most
radical one—let God take care of it. Do nothing.

Julie was pregnant the first month. We quickly
abandoned that position going forward.

Our daughter Ruth was born three months premature, weighing 2 lbs 5 oz, and she was quickly life-flighted from Stillwater to Tulsa. We went home, packed our things, and drove to St. Francis to meet her. She spent the next three months there, in the wonderful care of the nurses.

As far as we know, she's been gravid three more times since then. It's a miracle how women grow people inside of them. She doesn't do a good job of explaining to me what it's like or what it feels like. I wonder about that, the changes in her body as the baby grows, and then how it comes out, and then afterwards. I know it's common (353,000 every day), but it's no less amazing.

Anna, our youngest was born in August 2001, and I had a vasectomy before she was born. She's a junior in high school and about to leave the house to attend college soon.

Last fall, however, Julie's cycle was a bit wonky. I asked her about it, and she told me that according to her app tracker, she was nine days late. Nine days late! What?!

I pleaded with her to take a pregnancy test. I was freaking out. How can this happen? I'm 48. She's 47. Our youngest is 17. I mean, I know technically how it happen, but...

I couldn't think about anything else. There wasn't anything I could do, except know or not know. I couldn't affect the outcome. She was or she wasn't.

That was a strange few days.
Whew, not gravid again.

HAPPY

Circa 2006

Being married to me isn't easy. I'm a wild card. I've got my moods, my passion, my energy, my projects, my idiosyncrasies.

When we moved to Norman, Julie was seven-months' pregnant with Anna. We'd been living in my parents' basement for the six months since I'd graduated from Covenant Seminary. We bought our first house. I started a new job in ministry at the University of Oklahoma in Norman.

The first thing I had to do was Staff Training, which meant two full weeks in Atlanta with the other ten new campus ministers that were hired that year. That was a lot for her.

All that change. All those kids. All that cooking. All that blended-model partial homeschooling. All those people in the house. All those college students. All that husband sleep-walking, beer-brewing, game-playing.

We hit a low around 2012–2013. We were a few years into starting City Pres, and it was a struggle. Highs and lows, but the lows seemed lower. I was wondering if we could make it. She was too.

One of the things that helped—and I write this not saying this was the miracle cure, the silver bullet—was her diagnosis for depression. She'd resisted that. She wanted to be able to fix it. She describes how she felt as lying in a deep grave and unable to claw her way out. She wasn't sure if she wanted to even if she could.

The nurse practitioner prescribed some medication, which she'd been reluctant to take. But she did.

Praise Jesus. I'm so thankful. I'm sad that her brain chemistry and outlook had taken this turn, but that's the way things work sometimes.

I feel like I'm married to a different person than I was back then. A happier woman. One who is better able to handle the still-difficult things that come our way. A pill doesn't wipe away pain and suffering. It doesn't make either her or me make excellent decisions. But it sure does help the middle be much more stable and enjoyable.

INCORRECTNESS-ELIMINATOR

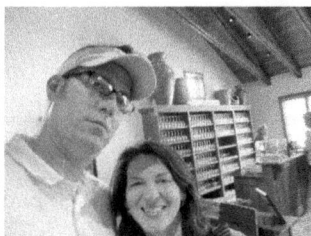

On an anniversary trip in West Texas

I know, I know. This isn't a word. So I'm cheating. I get it.

I'm trying to find a place to talk about how excellent of an editor Julie is. So this is my shot.

When we were in journalism school, I gravitated toward the creative writing side, and I tried to do the least amount possible. I'm not suggesting this is a positive character trait.

Julie was all in. She went the extra mile. She was in the newspaper room working on stories, just like all of the serious-minded students were. She was a whiz at editing.

That skill went underground to some extent with all those babies and moves, but it would resurface now and then. She edited for Covenant Seminary and their printed guidebooks. She had odd jobs here and there.

After we moved to OKC and our kids grew up a little bit, she made a move to start Storied Publishing. She began editing on the side for various projects in and around the city, especially for nonprofits and friends who needed help to tell their stories well.

We started White Blackbird Books out of a crisis in 2016. I'd been recruiting friends of my in our denomination to compile chapters in a book about racial reconciliation. We had a deadline because we had an important national meeting in June. My friend Sean was going to publish the book.

But Sean sold his business, and we found ourselves in the lurch. We quickly realized we had no other option for the book except to figure out how to publish it ourselves, something Julie had already suggested.

So we went for it.

I handed her the Word document, and she worked her MAGIC. Wow. She's so good.

I'm not sure if you realize how many things there are to know, and how many mistakes can be make. The Chicago Manual of Style is a big, technical book. I've tried to get better, but it's maddening to try to figure out how to fix all the incorrectness out there. Julie eliminates incorrectness. With style. With grace. With love. With serious-minded devotion. Bespeckled. Do not get in her way.

It's been fun learning more about her world and working together on projects so people can be heard in teh best way possible. She's a Jedi master.

JUVENAL

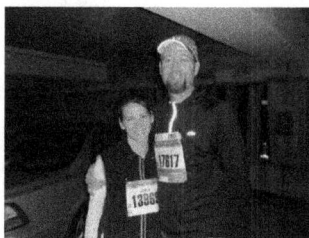

After a marathon or a half marathon

Juvenal means youthful, and I love to hear her laugh. I'll do a lot to get a laugh.

Lately, Julie has been setting her alarm for 7:15 a.m., but we've been staying in bed for 20–30 minutes. We snuggle. I try to get close to her, but it's most important to make her laugh.

I have a few standard jokes that I trot out now and then. I'll both get a laugh and an eye roll. But

I'm always coming up with new material. I assure you, it is hilarious.

She's been more serious-minded in the past, and she can be no doubt. But her big laugh, the belly laugh, the all-out cackle is something that brings joy to my life. That smile. She's the wife of my youth, and she keeps me young and guessing too. Our juvenal adventures together are sometimes silly, sometimes crazy, and usually fun.

PS: Juvenal was also the name of a Roman poet in and around 50 AD.

Julie does not appreciate that this is not a Webster's Dictionary-approved word.

So I can switch it to Juvenescenct.

KIND

On a hike in Colorado on vacation with the kids

Julie is kind.

I suppose I could stop there, but that doesn't seem like a full chapter or description.

She'll help you out. She had boundaries, yes, but you can test them, and you'll find they're far past what you might expect.

We've had people live with us over the years. A recently graduated college student, Russ, lived with us for over a year. He became a part of the family.

More recently, Nathan, Dominique, Ana, and

Grant have lived with us. We're considering opening our home to another friend we've met lately. Julie has talked about fostering children, and I cannot say no. I wonder who the Lord will put in our path over the next twenty-five years.

Her kindness is a part of who she is. I've already talked about her sass, and her foxiness, and her editing, but kindness is by far a greater quality. There are times when I try to tell her to be more mean, more ruthless, more cut-throat. She can't, and I love her for that. I've come to see that kindness as a Christ-likeness that I seek to emulate in her.

All the time, I see her go out of her way to serve others.

I love your sense of humor
I love to see you smile
I love your sense of balance
I love your sense of time
I love your music in the morning
Your rhythm in the night
But it's your kindness that shines so bright

I love your beauty
I love your sexy moves
More I love your honesty
You always tell the truth

I love your vision of the future
Your hope that never dies
But it's your kindness that clears my skies

I love your wisdom
Your knowledge of the past
Your willingness to listen
Your taste for what will last
I love your compassion for the suffering
And your solid happiness
But it's your kindness I love best
I love, I love, I love....
— David Wilcox, *Kindness*

LITERATE

Again in Colorado

When we were raising our kids, we got weirdly involved in a Classical Christian School. I say that because it wasn't in our upbringing or training. We were journalism/word/writing/editing people involved in Christian ministry at a public university.

I still don't know what to make of it. It was a wild time. The school is great. It's not something I'd have predicted we'd have done.

A part of classical education (google a famous

essay by Dorothy Sayers) is learning the rules, the repetition of it all, the foundation of learning. Think addition and subtraction tables, history facts, and grammar rules. Every parent (and by that I mean every mom) learned how to drill their children in grammar rules with grammar ditties in grammar perfection.

Somewhere along the way, Julie realized that this could help more than the children in our care, the ones she'd given birth to. She started volunteering to help illiterate adults in Norman (see: kind). She'd meet them at the library and go over the same grammar facts and ditties she'd been teaching our kids. Lightbulbs came on. Lives were altered.

She loves literacy. She ended up going back to school at Mizzou to get a Master's in English Education. She taught learning skills at Oklahoma City Community School, a last stop for students who were not doing well, usually for some sort of undiagnosed learning disorder. She was a master at it.

She began volunteering her time at a local elementary school. Our state requires students to pass a reading test in third grade. If they don't past, they cannot matriculate. But the students are often first-generation English speakers whose parents are not proficient in English, don't have time to read to them, and are trying desperately to make ends' meet. She worked with the school to identify the students who were not going to pass, but with some help might be able to. She organized volunteers to read with those students one-on-one for thirty minutes on Fridays.

It's made a tremendous difference.

She's a hero.

Now she works with the Oklahoma City Metro Literacy Coalition helping to promote literacy in our city.

Reading—it's a simple, misunderstood step in personal development. Most of us can—you're reading this book so you've got it. If you cannot, then you are at a disadvantage in life. We can do this. Julie is helping. I'm so proud of her. The kingdom of God is at work in these mustard seed moments.

MACADAMIZER*

In Mexico with family, summer of 2010

Macadamize to make roads with tiny pebbles.

I'm thinking about how Julie and I have forged this pathway together these now twenty-five years. We have miles and miles through the woods and plains together.

Tiny pebbles of forgiveness asked for and granted. We've gotten better and faster at forgiveness. "I'm sorry, please forgive me" used to be more difficult to say. "I forgive you" tougher to give.

We'd store up anger and resentment, trying to

pave our road by ignoring our hearts and keeping away from the pain.

We wanted to be a perfect couple, the ideal husband and wife, man and woman. Perfect couples don't fight, so that was off limits. Our solution was to stew, simmer, and retract.

We've learned that we cannot be each others' saviors. We can't make everything fine for the other person all the time. I can't fix her. She cannot fix me.

But we can walk together and be for each other. We can pave a windy road together with these pebbles:

I'm sorry. Please forgive me.

I forgive you.

Julie has made walking the road of life much richer for me.

———

* Not the original m word

NOMOGRAPHER

*RUF '80s party—circa 2007—we were named
king and queen*

A nomographer writes the rules.

When we were engaged, we ended up at
Dillards to register for our wedding gifts. Back then
you didn't do this online. You didn't have a bar-
code-scanner gun to upload your choices. You had a
lady following your around in real time recording
your choices on paper to print up in a report.

That was the day I realized we had different
ideas about how to build a household. I didn't

know I had these opinions on dishes, towels, bedspreads, and kitchen items. I'm not sure where I got them. However, I soon learned that this was a conflict I was not going to win 100 percent.

Although I did succeed in no flowers on our plates, I lost that same "battle" on the bedspread. 100 percent flowers. I realized this was not a good fight to fight. The bedspread still kept us warm.

Every marriage is a third culture. We're all melding our upbringings and our ideas into something new. Halbert-ness and Serven-ness intertwine into something that had never been seen in the world before. What would it look like?

How would we do Thanksgiving? —Our first one married was at Bennigan's in Tulsa. Non ideal.

How would we do Christmas? —Our first one was at a hotel in Tulsa because Ruth was about to get out of the hospital.

How would we do the Super Bowl? —Our first one Ruth was home, and we didn't have a tv at our house, and I was committed to not making a big deal out of it, so I remember we went grocery shopping during the Super Bowl.

What are the rules?

For cleanliness? For eating? For snacking? For soda? For homework? For who takes care of the car? For buying groceries? For church attendance? For girlfriends and boyfriends? For who gets to watch a movie at how old and for why?

One of my favorite "Rules" nomographer instances comes in two parts.

1) Bad words are somewhat tricky. Cox or cocks? We import meanings into syllables asperated by our mouths. In our house, one of the worst things anyone could say was, of all things, "eyeball."

This seems insane looking back on it. Cal and Drew would say the word "eyeball" and Anna would lose her lid. It was a war. So naturally, they'd say it a million times. It was funny in some sense because obviously "eyeball" is not a bad word. But it didn't matter. There was no real reasoning. "Eyeball" was banned.

That only fanned the eyeball flames.

2) A rule was enacted that "bad words" were not to be uttered. This makes a certain amount of sense. We don't need to be vulgar for its own sake. We can show restraint.

But the kids figured out that there were rules around the rules, the nomographer had standards.

So is "enis" the same as "penis"? "einer" instead of "weiner"? "upid" instead of "stupid"?

Words started without the first letter or syllable seems to get a pass, so that was a whole language that rose up, and it still gets used to this day.

"oobies."

"esticles."

"ig ummy."

You get it.

Rule followers lead to rule breakers.

O WORDS

Actual profession photo shoot, 2012

For O, I opened up the voting to see what the people had to say. Here were the results:

Opulent—This means luxurious or lavish. I'd put this in the category of beautiful, but she doesn't have expensive taste. I usually get in trouble if I spend money. She's opulent to me.

Outstanding—Without a doubt, Julie is outstanding. All the time, I'm meeting people who say, "Oh, you're Julie's husband." Yep, that's me.

Original—She's an OG definitely. No one else like her.

Observant—I'm guessing this is a reference to Julie's editing skills. She's the best. I don't know how she finds errors like she does. It's impressive.

Omnivorous—I believe this to be true, but this doesn't seem especially noteworthy.

Outrageous—Outrageous seems to be a stretch to me. I think she is, but she doesn't show this side of herself to everyone.

Omniscient—Julie is a wise sage. She knows an awful lot. She can peer into your soul. Watch out.

Obliging—She's willing to give you the benefit of the doubt unless you're a dog and your name is Charlie and you live in our house and she thinks you've peed on the carpet. Then you're done for.

Orthodox—She is a Presbyterian after all. Decently and in order.

Overachiever—Yes. We had a class in college that we both signed up pass fail instead of getting a letter grade. I got a C—, so I passed. She got an A, so she passed. I tried to tell her she played the game wrong.

Oxygen—I'm not sure how to spin this.

Osmosis—?

Optimus Prime—A Transformer. Julie is one of our church's pastors'/elders' wives. This group of women formed right around when the Mob Wives tv show was on. I love that show. I'd joke that when they got together for dinner once a month, there was all this drama, back biting, and hair pulling.

Obedient—This was supposed to be a joke, but she is obedient. To God. To the rules. To her friends. And even to me sometimes.

Optimistic—She's gotten better at this one, so I could see it now.

Ornery—This is a word her mom uses to describe her, and it's accurate.

Open-minded—She's changed her views on many topics since we've known each other, and so have I.

We like to have fearless conversations. We hope to risk to rescue as we pursue prodigals.

Olly olly oxen free—Kudos to the most original. This is a reference that people feel free around her. That's true.

Omnidirectional—Julie can accomplish many different tasks, and she can also focus on completing one at a time. She's multifaceted.

PULCHRITUDINOUS

Before Ruth's wedding, July 2018. Don't worry I wore a suit too.

I don't believe I've mentioned yet how straight out pulchritudinous she is. 100 percent pulchritude.

That means beautiful and beauty. I did talk about this back at Foxy, but I'm returning to the subject.

Once for about six months, I didn't like how she'd cut her hair, but that's about it. I'm racking my brain to think of specific times I didn't think she was beautiful, and I'm having a difficult time.

We've been talking about the different iterations of each other. I've been married to at least three different women, all of them Julie Serven.

We change over the years. Newly married. New mom. Watching little kids. Kids growing up. Kids leaving and getting married themselves.

Like many women, Julie felt stuck at home with children. She loved and hated it. She wasn't sure what she was good at doing, what her tastes were, and how she could best engage in the world around her.

I didn't always know how to help and support her. I did the best I could to encourage her to be the woman God made her to be, but I couldn't make that happen for her.

We've been changing and growing. I'd rather be 48 than 28, and she'd say the same. This is a much better stage of life.

Julie 3.0 likes life more. That gets us back to Happy. Bespeckled Julie is Foxy, Mammiferous, and Pulchritudinous. That's something that hasn't changed in the various versions, but it comes out more and more, better and better.

QUIDDLE

Big Cedar Lodge, circa 2007

A quiddle is a fastidious person. This is a bit of a stretch in regard to Julie, but it'll have to do.

When we were first married, Julie had years of adult living under her belt. I had nearly zero. I spent four years in the dorms during college, and really only had my first place in Stillwater from August until we were married in March.

Not only that but back then especially I was the most disorganized person on the planet. I don't know how I graduated from Mizzou with the way I structured my tine and what I needed to get done.

Julie became the organized one. That's funny now because the truth was she just was more organized than me. The bar was low for sure. But it helped that she had an idea about where to put things, how to plan a day or a meal or going to the grocery store. My strategy was to walk around without even making a list. I'd get home, unpack, and then make several trips back to the store as I discovered what I'd forgotten. Not picture perfect efficiency.

I don't think we were tipped off in our premarital counseling that our fights would consist of these types of daily encounters.

We had a baby in the hospital, and we lived below the poverty line. We were house-sitting, and I was involved in full-time ministry.

But we fought about where to put the dishes. We fought about toothpaste and soap placement. We fought about how I'd always forget to close the pantry door.

I've gotten better, and she's gotten more chill. We've created more of our own third culture, and not everything is worth fighting about. Eh. Okay, let's do it that way. Sometimes we do it my way, too. It's okay to be fastidious about some things. We let a ton go too. Quiddle.

RED

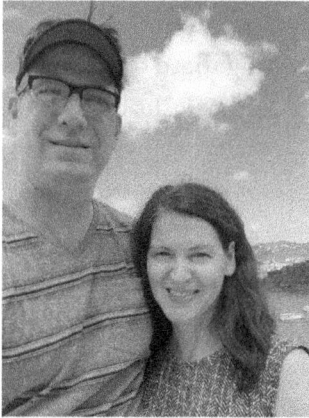

On a sailing trip, 2016

Within the last month, I found out her favorite
color is red.

Did I already know that?

I was buying a gift for her, and it involved two

color choices. I thought I'd get our two favorite colors.

Mine—gray.

When did this gray thing start? My best guess is it's when I first signed up for one of those clothes delivery companies three or so years ago. My wardrobe needed an update, and I hated doing the shopping. They'd send me more fashionable clothes each month. Win. There were two choices for color schemes. One was the more colorful, out there colors, and the other was more black, gray, and white.

At the time I went for the basics.

I started getting those three colors every month, and the gray was the easiest. Everything goes with gray.

Somewhere along the way the kids and Julie noticed that it was gray every day. I'll keep them on their toes with some black and white every now and then, but I'm a fan of the gray (I bought us gray sheets for the bed for Christmas, and they're glorious).

Julie—hm.

I guess teal. I think I've seen her in an aqua or teal if I mentally scan her wardrobe. Mostly different shaded of blue. But was I right?

No. It's red.

I called the gift company back and changed my order.

A favorite color is a basic information point. It's

good to re-ask now and then. I like to know what her favorite things are, and I also like to throw her a curveball when I can.

Kristy knows her favorite tea at Urban Tea House, so I get that.

She has a favorite place to get a massage.

She has a favorite coffee mug (does she?).

She has a favorite color, and it is red.

SIFFLEUR

At Glacier National Park, circa 2004

Siffleur is a fancy word for someone who is a professional whistler. I'm not sure what a professional whistler is, but Julie is not qualified.

I'm listing something she's not. She cannot whistle.

I'd think that with enough time and practice anyone could learn to whistle, but at this point that ship has sailed.

Sometimes we learn from not only what we are, but also by what we're not.

Not tall.

Not male.

Not a person of color.

Not extroverted.

Not single.

Not rude.

Not a fan of sriracha.

Not unwilling to watch the Cardinals with her husband, or at least be in the room doing something else while the game is on.

Not especially interested in the Sooners.

Not going to drive a stick shift.

Not ready to go gray.

Not particular about her husband's facial hair.

Not yet a grandmother.

Not excited about leaving her seventeen-year-old daughter by herself at the house while we go to Florida on a short vacation.

Not a siffleur.

PS - My mother would like to enter the word "Saint" for Julie for being married to me this long. That's fair. Julie has some stuff to put up with, no doubt.

TOOKIE BEAR

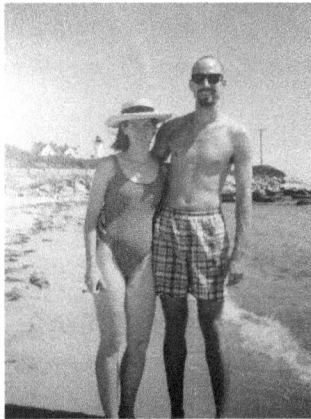

On our five-year-anniversary vacation in Cape Cod, 1998

Pet names and nicknames are funny things. They get attached to you, and they morph over time.

Our first pet name was "Pootie Pie." I'm nearly 100 percent positive this came from a Calvin and Hobbes cartoon.

Calvin: I'm never going to get married. Are you?

Hobbes: Hm. I suppose if the right person comes along, I might. Somebody with green eyes and a nice laugh, who I could call "Pooty Pie."

Calvin: "Pooty Pie?"

Hobbes: Or "Bitsy Pookums."

Calvin: I think that would affect my stomach a lot more than my heart.

Hobbes: "Bitsy Pookums," I'd say. Yes, "Snoogy Woogy," she'd say.

So, that settled it. I'd found my right person, with green eyes, and a nice laugh. My Pootie Pie (we changed the spelling). That even made it into my vows to her.

[An aside: Writing your own vows is a terrible idea. I don't let any of the couples I marry do it. They say the traditional vows, and then if they'd like they can have a second set and do whatever they want.

I Doug, take you, Julie, to be my wedded wife. And I do promise before God, and these witnesses, that I will be true to you, forsaking all others, keeping myself only for you, from this day forward, to have and to hold, to love and to cherish, to honor and protect, in the midst of all God brings to us, so long as we both shall live.

I Julie, take you Doug, to be my wedded

husband. And I do promise before God, and these witnesses, that I will be true to you, forsaking all others, keeping myself only for you, from this day forward, to have and to hold, to love and to cherish, to honor and serve, in the midst of all God brings to us, so long as we both shall live.

These vows have stood the test of time. They're not effectual per se, but they pack a punch. You're vowing up ahead into the future, into times when you're going to want to quit and give up. Return to these vows and keep trying to stick it out.]

Somewhere along the way, this changed to Tookie Bear, and then Tookie, and then Took.

And we called our kids the Tookies.

It's stayed steady for quite awhile now, but perhaps it will take a different form. I doubt we'll land on Bitsy Pookums, but don't hold me to it.

I love you Tookie Bear. You're my Pootie Pie.

URBANIST

On a trip, circa 2015

In 2011, we moved from Norman, Oklahoma, thirty miles up the road to Oklahoma City.

I started working on our new church (City Presbyterian Church) in June, but we didn't move until October. Starting a new church is hard, hard work. I'd drive back and forth from Norman to OKC sometimes three times a day.

I told Julie that even though I hated having to do that, I didn't have the energy to put into house-hunting and moving. I'd leave it up to her, but I thought it was a bad idea to move until the church was up and running.

She'd come up with lists. We didn't know much about the city, or where the church would end up locating. Norman is fairly self-contained small city with a definite identity. Since our kids were small, ministry took time, and Norman had all we needed, we rarely had ventured up to OKC.

Another factor in our lack of OKC excursions was that OKC wasn't like it is now. It's been growing in places to go and eat. It's way cooler now than it used to be.

We were in the dark. I didn't want to look.

Julie took the reins, and she made lists, and talked to me about it.

We ended up in the best house, in a perfect neighborhood for us. It was a minor miracle.

The listers had decided to go into a Make Me Move site. If we wanted them to move, we'd pay the price they wanted. Otherwise, they'd stay.

When we walked in the door the first day we saw the house, I knew the husband. Tommy! We'd played basketball in the rec center at OU for years.

We bought the house, and we've been exploring ever since. We're more interested in local government, politics, and schools. We love to visit the new restaurants we can walk to. We're fully invested in the shalom of Oklahoma City.

Good job, Urbanist. I'm glad I get to live here with her.

Uxorial—pertaining to a wife.

Uxorious—fond of one's wife.

VIRTUOUS & VIGILANT

With Ruth and Cal, circa 1997

I don't know of a better person. I'm not exaggerating.

Patient.

Kind.

Loving.

Faithful.

Good.

Loving.

Merciful.

Generous.

Willing.

Studious.

Temperate.

I could go on and on.

What more could you ask for? Yes, yes, she's a sinner. She has her faults. We all do. There is room for improvement. That's the beauty of sanctification: God's not done yet. We're getting closer and closer to what Jesus wants us to be. We're dying to the flesh, and we're living to the Spirit. Old Julie is less. New Julie is more.

I know she makes me a better person. Being connected to her is the best decision I've made. Sticking it out with her even better.

For the first time, I'm going to officially through in a second word, and that is Vigilant.

If we want to go even further, then I'll add Verucca, which is a word for warts.

Julie hates warts. That's not especially noteworthy. No one likes warts, but she's on the warpath against them.

We spent the summer in Acapulco in 2010.

We volunteered at an orphanage, and I was in charge of the American interns who came down to help there.

One day, we were in our apartment talking to the boys, and I think she screamed. Cal was thirteen, and his foot was nearly completely covered in one huge wart. I suppose we hadn't seen his feet in awhile, and perhaps he hadn't either.

It was mammoth.

That set us on a pathway to checking for, finding, and eliminating warts. Doctors visits. Cutting them out. Freezing them off. Shooting them with drugs to kill them.

Warts spread. They're evil. They're like sin in that they don't just go away. If you ignore them, they can get much worse.

Consider this a Public Service Announcement from Julie and on her behalf: Get rid of the warts. Be vigilant.

WAYGONE

In Florida at RUF Summer Conference, circa
2004

Waygone is a word that means exhausted from travels.

When we were getting married, we didn't have a place secured to live until about two weeks beforehand. I can't remember what the hold up was, but that isn't the greatest plan. It all worked out, and God came through for us in a big way.

We lived in Stillwater, and I worked for The Navigators for three years. During that time with

Ruth in the hospital, my theological bearings shifted significantly, and I became unhappy doing what I was doing. I wanted to go to seminary to study.

I announced that that was what we were going to do. I was headed to Covenant Seminary in St. Louis. I didn't know what the final outcome would be, and I didn't know how I would pay for it, but we were committed.

However, that summer, I had already said we'd help with a Summer Training Program in Colorado Springs, so I wanted to fulfill that. We packed our stuff, and we moved full on out to the Springs. We put all of our belongings in storage.

During those few months, I came to realization that there was no way I could pay for seminary. I had no idea how that would happen.

We were asked if we'd consider staying in the Springs and worked at a college there. We said yes. It would be a new work, and we'd be on the ground floor.

Then the staff member who had asked us told us he wasn't going to do that after all. What? Not my fault.

We started negotiating with The Navigators, who were gracious and patient with us. We ended up getting placed in Lincoln, Nebraska at the University of Nebraska. We moved all of our belonging to Lincoln, our second full move in three months. Stillwater-Colorado Springs-Lincoln.

Julie was pregnant with Cal. He was delivered in Lincoln on a freezing cold day in late November.

By that time I had realized I couldn't do it. There was no way I could invest time getting settled in Lincoln for years before I went to seminary.

I still didn't know how I'd pay for it, but I had to get to St Louis and start at Covenant. I finished out the school year, and we moved again. If you're keeping track that's four places, with three full moves in approximately fifteen months.

I didn't know where to land the plane. I had all these choices. I was in my mid twenties. I didn't know what I wanted to do. I'd already had two kids, and we were both unhappy. I'd never planned on being a pastor. We were broke. But we were broke at Covenant Seminary in St Louis in June 1997.

We lived in the same apartment there for a full, steady, three and a half years. We moved to Norman and lived in the same house for ten full years. We've now lived in the same house in Oklahoma City for coming up on eight years. Doing better! The plane has stabilized!

This is a book about marriage and about Julia. Not about me.

Julie, I'm sure you were wondering if we'd ever figure it out. Those first years were insane. I'm sorry. Thank you for hanging in there with me. We made it. It's gotten better.

XENODOCIAL

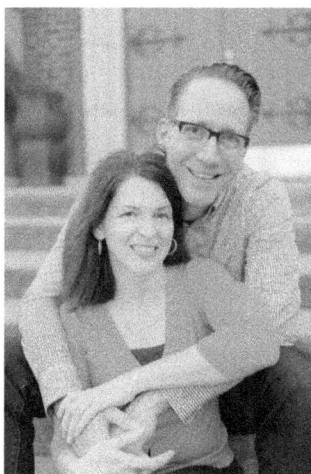

2016

A person who is hospitable and kind to strangers is considered xenodochial. That's Julie.

One of our friends I'll call Victoria. Julie met her one Sunday when she showed up at church on accident. She'd meant to go somewhere else, but got off at the wrong stop and found City Pres, and she walked in. The first person she met was Julie, who happened to be greeting that day.

Julie took her to lunch after church, and she heard Victoria's story. Other people might have stopped there, but Julie keeps pressing in, keeps up the good fight, keeps in contact.

We ended up a year later at Victoria's apartment rescuing her and her boys from her abusive husband. They moved in. Victoria stayed with us until we could find her her own place.

We were blessed by her. Not only her smile, but also her tears. Not only her Spanish, but her tamales graciously, meticulously cooked for us. Her persistence to love her boys well, no matter what. She's no longer a stranger; she's a good, good friend.

Julie and I had gotten into a place where nearly all of our friends looked and lived just like us. At the time we didn't know how sad that was. How restricted.

Since then our worlds have opened up into brighter colors, languages, tastes, and experiences. It's far better.

If she were to say we're going to foster, I'd know we're in all the way. If we're going to host new strangers, they'll become friends soon enough.

Julie loves this, and so do I.

YIPS & YIKES

2016

Julie is petrified of getting sniffed or bit by catfish in the lake. I don't think this has ever happened to her, but if she's in the water, she's thinking about it and talking about it. The whole time.

Julie always thinks she smells something. No one else can smell it, but she's positive she can. Perhaps this is a super power?

In the same vein, she thinks everyone can hear everything. We can be talking in our upstairs bedroom, and she asks me to lower my voice because our next-door neighbor might hear us. I don't think she can. I'm positive she can't (she's also in her eighties).

She used to get spooked when I'd come to bed at night. It's me.

She's a terrible back seat driver. She thinks I'm going to run into everything she sees. She'll gasp and grab my arm, which nearly causes me to wreck when I wasn't even close to what she saw.

Our son Drew has two tricks that make her crazy. One is his smoker's laugh. She counters with a high-pitched cackle. Then he'll hug her from behind, putting his arms around her stomach. She cannot stand this, but the fatal flaw is when he realized her displeasure. So that activity ramped up.

She was afraid of my dad for years when they first met, while she starting coming around, even after we got married. He intimidated her. Then she figured him out.

On the one hand, I try to mitigate against these yips and these yikes. On the other hand, I'd love to see a real live catfish bite her in the ass. Just once.

ZYGOTES

City Pres photo booth

I'm to Z already. I could go back through again, but it's time to end.

For this last entry, I'd like to talk about our four kids, and two of them are married, so there are six total to discuss. I've mentioned each of them along the way. Our lives are now wrapped up into theirs.

Ruth lives in Charlottesville with her husband, Adam. They were married in July 2018 (I can't come up with the exact date off the top of my head). She's a newspaper reporter (journalism at

Mizzou!), and Adam is moving towards physics. Ruth has that amazing story of being born three months early and weighing so little. She's a fighter. And a writer. She and Adam are incredible separately, and even better together.

Cal lives in Oklahoma City with his wife, Mady. They were married January 13, 2019. Both of them are involved in social media, communication, and film. He's also a writer, and he's working on a novel. Cal is fiercely loyal to his friends. He's hilarious but in a sneaky way. You've got to hang in there for a while. We're thrilled with Mady. We love her so much, and we're so thankful she's in our lives. She's a delight, not only to him but to us.

Drew is currently (2019) a freshman at Cornell. He's studying economics, but his real deal is rowing. He rows and rows. He's great at math, but he won't talk about that. He talks about rowing. We'll see where God leads him. He's a great, great son and the hardest worker you've ever seen. We're so proud of him.

Anna is our baby girl who is now seventeen. She's a junior in high school. She's devoted, funny, kind, and usually pretty patient. She's determined. She's figuring out her next steps and how to combine her college choice with rowing. She's not hated being the last one in the house with just the two of us.

They each have different stories. They're variant in personalities, outlooks, and pathways.

Julie has been the best mom they could have asked for. We've made our mistakes and life has ups and downs. We didn't know what we were doing with parenting, school, discipline, church, conflict, existential questions, friend drama, dating, allowances, moving, family dinners, or anything really.

We took some sweet family vacations, and that created great memories and iPhoto books to remember them by.

We have family meetings where we discussed weighty matters ranging from moving to OKC to the great unmatched sock mystery.

We attended events like OU football games and wrestling matches, U2 concerts, ski trips, Okie Noodling Festival, General Assembly, weightlifting competitions, baseball games, soccer games, volleyball games, games, games, games, concerts that were terrible, school plays, end of year festivals, the Medieval Fair, and many more.

We listened to good music: Sufjan Stevens, Patty Griffith, Indelible Grace, Johnny Cash, Toby Keith, Willie Nelson, Jack Johnson, and whatever Anna put on Pandora (usually country or pop).

We had good times on the porch with our friends in Norman. And in our house in OKC outside by the fire pit.

We saw those naked dudes at that clothing-optional swimming hole in New Mexico that one time. That was weird.

We played games: Agricola, Dominion, Puerto Rico, Dutch Blitz, Mexican dominoes, Power Grid, Beans, and lately Gizmos and Azul.

We watched our fair share of tv: Barney (no!), Sesame Street, 24, West Wing, Gilmore Girls, Impractical Jokers, CNN, and whatever Food Network Show is on.

We've done homeschool, private school, public school, and charter school.

We've read books together: all of those school books, Harry Potter, Magic Bus books, Promise and Deliverance, Love Does, and many more.

We've been members of churches, serving them as best we could.

There was that one time Anna erased all of Cal's progress on the video game he'd been working on for months.

I cut the boys' hair, and they hated that.

We wrestled. We played snow football. We played catch in the yard for hours.

We sold food for the Rainy Day Cafe.

We threw up in the parking lot, threw fits, threw temper tantrums, threw the football.

We had tea parties, and we built legos for hours.

We've sung hymns, prayed psalms, and recited creeds.

We love the St Louis Cardinals, the OU Sooners, and the Oklahoma Sooners. We have loved the Mizzou Tigers in the past, but then they joined the SEC, and that just isn't going to work.

We paid for an awful lot of school.

We've gone over homework, teaching and grading.

We've prayed hours and hours.

We've cut the grass, painted the fence, jumped on the trampoline, cleaned the bathroom, fixed the phone, washed the sheets, cried the tears, thrown the parties, and opened the presents.

Our stories are intertwined with our parents: Fred and his wife Della, Jeanie, Dan and Donna. Our sisters, half sisters, and step siblings. Our nieces and nephews. Our long-time and newly found friends.

All for the glory of God. It's our chief end: to glorify God and enjoy him forever.

CONCLUSION

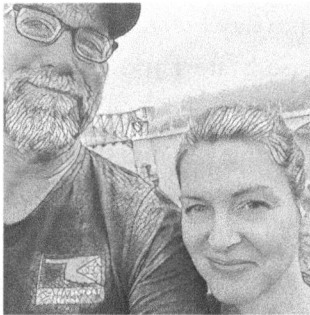

In Chattanooga at a regatta, 2017

I don't know what lies ahead.

During one counseling session with Bruce in Dallas, Julie casually started a sentence this way: "Well, when we get divorced...." Then she continued.

Wait? What?

When we get divorced?

I'd never heard her say she assumed we would get divorced someday. That's what people do.

I understand that reality, but it's not my worldview. It's not where I go. I tend to be more future positive, and my parents are still married fifty years later.

There were some days/weeks/months/years perhaps where I started to wonder. I didn't think it was fair for her to be so unhappy married to me. I knew plenty of couples who stuck it out just based on principle alone. They hated their marriage, but doggone it, they were committed.

There was a day I went out for a hike by myself at Roman Nose State Park. I had a Coke Zero, a Subway sandwich, a book, a journal, and a lawn chair I could sling on my shoulders like a back pack. I wandered into the park, and found a stream to sit by. I thought, prayed, read, and wrote.

Then I got lost. I could see where I wanted to go off in the distance, but I couldn't get there. I'd start toward it, but the trail would change, and I'd take a wrong switchback, and end up going the opposite way I intended. I was dehydrated. It was a 90-degree October day. I wasn't really worried, but I also wasn't sure what was going to happen in the next few hours.

During that time, God talked to me. I believe this to be true. Through the Bible, the sacraments, prayer, and people. And every once and awhile straight up to me.

He said very plainly and simply, "It's going to be okay." My dehydration? My path back to my car? My marriage? What's going to be okay, God?

"It's going to be okay."

It's going to be okay doesn't mean smooth sailing with no whammies. There will be ups and downs. We'll have rocky roads. We'll have troubled waters. We'll have fights at times. We'll disagree. We'll get off kilter and out of sync. We won't always be on the same page.

But it'll be okay. Team Serven.

I know 25 years has been better than any other, so I have hope, and I think she does too. We'll keep on plugging away and see where we end up. Abrosial to Zygotes and everywhere in between.

Here's the next 25!

www.ingramcontent.com/pod-product-compliance
Lightning Source LLC
Chambersburg PA
CBHW070116070426
42448CB00040B/2967